Awesome Asian Animals

Orangutans Are Awesome!

by Allan Morey

Consultant: Jackie Gai, DVM
Wildlife Veterinarian
Vacaville, California

CAPSTONE PRESS
a capstone imprint

A+ Books are published by Capstone Press,
1710 Roe Crest Drive, North Mankato, Minnesota 56003
www.capstonepub.com

Library of Congress Cataloging-in-Publication Data
Morey, Allan, author.
Orangutans are awesome! / by Allan Morey.
pages cm. — (A+ books. Awesome Asian animals)
Summary: "Introduces young readers to orangutans, including physical characteristics, habitat, diet, behavior,
and life cycle"— Provided by publisher.
Audience: Ages 4–8.
Audience: K to grade 3.
Includes bibliographical references and index.
ISBN 978-1-4914-3907-4 (library binding)
ISBN 978-1-4914-3926-5 (paperback)
ISBN 978-1-4914-3936-4 (eBook PDF)
1. Orangutans—Juvenile literature. I. Title.
QL737.P96M673 2016
599.88'3—dc23   2014045604

Editorial Credits
Michelle Hasselius, editor; Peggie Carley, designer; Tracy Cummins, media researcher;
Morgan Walters, production specialist

Photo Credits
Capstone Press, 6; FLPA: Alain Compost/Biosphoto, 7 Top, 11 Bottom, 28; Minden Pictures: Anup Shah, 1, 8, 13,
Cyril Ruoso, 18, Konrad Wothe, 19, Suzi Eszterhas, 29 Bottom; Shutterstock: Creativa Images, Cover Back, Eric
Isselee, Cover Top Left, Cover Bottom Right, hadkhanong, 27, jeep2499, Cover Top Right, Kjersti Joergensen, 15,
17, 22, Matej Hudovernik, 4, 7 Bottom Right, Michael Steden, Cover Bottom Left, Nagel Photography, 7 Bottom
Left, Peter Wollinga, 12, Rich Carey, 26 Bottom, Rigamondis, Design Element, Sergey Uryadnikov, 10, 30, tristan
tan, 29 Top; Thinkstock: Anup Shah, 21, Arturo Limon, 26 Top, edenwithin, 14, Eric Gevaert, 20, Eugene Junying
Sim, 23, GlobalP, 32, Goddard_Photography, 5, 25, istock, 9, Marci Paravia, 16, Mickrick, 24, Zoonar RF, 11 Top

Note to Parents, Teachers, and Librarians
This Awesome Asian Animals book uses full color photographs and a nonfiction format to introduce
the concept of orangutans. *Orangutans Are Awesome!* is designed to be read aloud to a pre-reader or
to be read independently by an early reader. Photographs help listeners and early readers understand
the text and concepts discussed. The book encourages further learning by including the following
sections: Table of Contents, Glossary, Read More, Internet Sites, Critical Thinking Using the Common
Core, and Index. Early readers may need assistance using these features.

Printed in China.
042015   008864WMF15

Table of Contents

Amazing Orangutans

Not all large animals live on the ground in a rain forest. Sometimes you have to look up. That's where orangutans spend most of their time. They are the largest animals living in the treetops.

Great Apes

Orangutans are only found in southeast Asia. They live on two islands—Sumatra and Borneo.

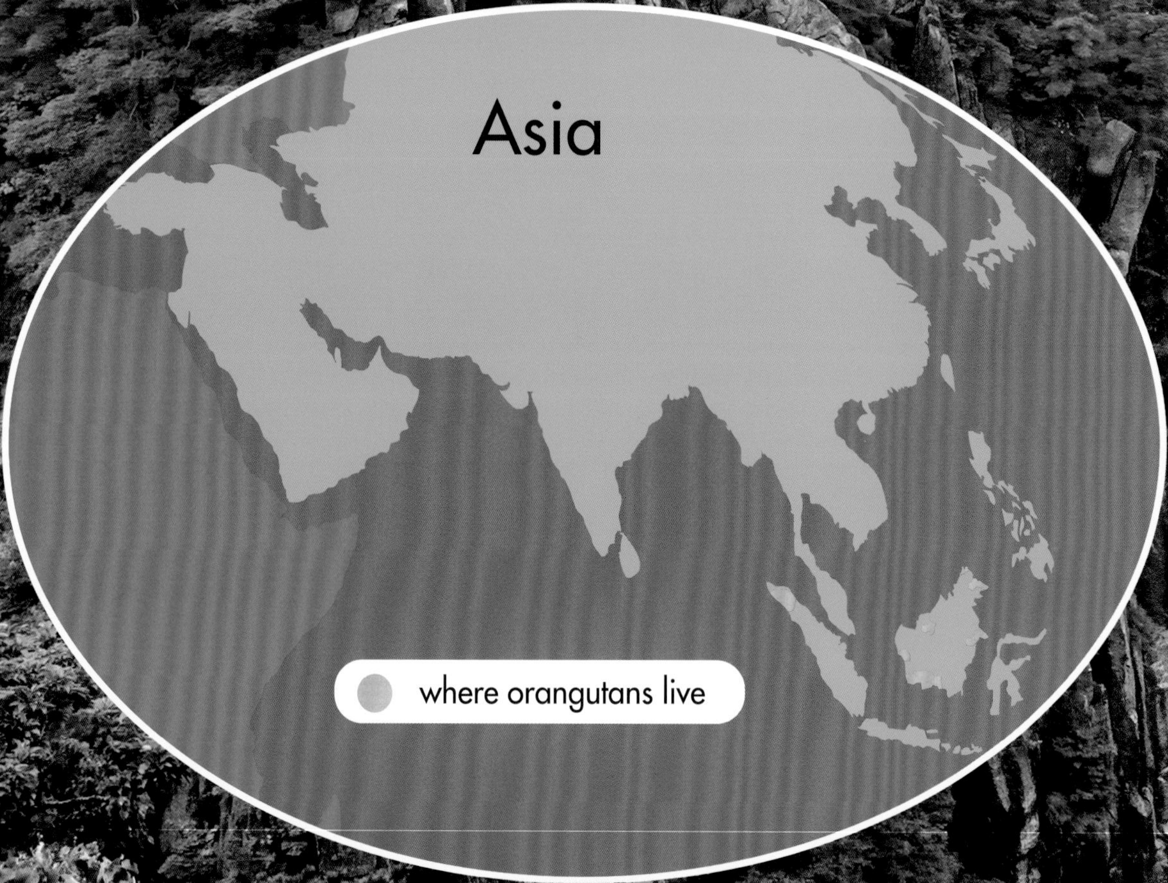

Asia

where orangutans live

Orangutans are one of the great apes. This group includes chimpanzees, bonobos, and gorillas. Animals that belong to this group are smart. Some can use tools to find food. Others can grasp items with their hands and feet.

Orangutans have shaggy red fur. That's why some people call them red apes.

Male orangutans don't look the same as females. They are much larger. Males have fatty cheek pads on the sides of their faces. Pouches hang from their throats. Some males even grow beards.

Male orangutans can weigh more than 200 pounds (91 kilograms). They can grow more than 4 feet (1.2 meters) tall. Because of their size, males travel on the ground more often than females.

Up in the Trees

Female orangutans can weigh up to 100 pounds (45 kg). They stand about 3 feet (0.9 m) tall.

Female orangutans build nests in trees.
They make nests out of branches and leaves.
Females share the nests with their young.

Orangutans have long arms. When standing straight up, an orangutan can touch the ground with its hands. A male can stretch its arms 7 feet (2.1 m) wide, from fingertip to fingertip.

Orangutans are very strong. They can hang from a tree branch by just one hand.

Fruit and Insects

Munch! Munch! Orangutans are omnivores. They eat plants and other animals. But orangutans mostly eat plants. They climb around the forest looking for fruit. If they can't find fruit, orangutans will eat leaves and bark. Orangutans will also eat ants, caterpillars, and termites. They may even eat fish.

Male orangutans spend most of their time alone. Males have territories where they search for food. To keep other males out of its territory, a male orangutan will shout. This shout can be heard more than 1 mile (1.6 kilometers) away. Males also call out to nearby females when it's time to mate.

Growing Up

A female orangutan usually gives birth to one baby at a time. For the first year of its life, a baby orangutan clings to its mother. It is not strong enough to climb through the trees on its own. After about two years, it will begin to play and swing on trees.

A young orangutan spends seven to eight years with its mother. During this time it learns what to eat and how to stay safe.

Even after it has left its mother, a young
orangutan may stay close to other orangutans.
It watches them to learn how to behave.

Saving Orangutans

Orangutans can live up to 40 years in the wild. Because orangutans live in trees, they are safe from most predators. The only time orangutans might be in danger is when they are on the ground. Then a tiger could pounce on them.

People are the biggest danger to orangutans. People chop down trees and destroy forests where orangutans live. They may also turn the forests into farmland. Some people even capture young orangutans to sell as pets.

Many people want to save orangutans. Wildlife groups work to protect them. In some countries there are laws against selling orangutans as pets. Parklands have been created so orangutans can live safely. Hopefully these awesome apes will always swing through the treetops.

Glossary

cheek pad (CHEEK PAD)—a fold of skin on an animal's face

mate (MATE)—to join together to produce young

omnivore (OM-nuh-vor)—an animal that eats plants and other animals

parkland (PARK-land)—land with trees and bushes that is or could be used as a park

pouch (POWCH)—a flap of skin that looks like a pocket

predator (PRED-uh-tur)—an animal that hunts other animals for food

termite (TUR-mite)—an antlike insect that eats wood

territory (TER-uh-tor-ee)—an area of land that an animal claims as its own to live in

Read More

Ganeri, Anita. *Orangutan.* A Day in the Life: Rain Forest Animals. Chicago: Heinemann Library, 2011.

Owen, Ruth. *Orangutans.* The World's Smartest Animals. New York: PowerKids Press, 2012.

Sabatino, Michael. *Being an Orangutan.* Can You Imagine? New York: Gareth Stevens Publishing, 2014.

Internet Sites

FactHound offers a safe, fun way to find Internet sites related to this book. All of the sites on FactHound have been researched by our staff.

Here's all you do:
Visit *www.facthound.com*
Type in this code: 9781491439074

Super-cool stuff! Check out projects, games and lots more at **www.capstonekids.com**

Critical Thinking Using the Common Core

1. Orangutans are one of the great apes. Name two other animals that belong to this group. (Key Ideas and Details)

2. Orangutans are omnivores. What does it mean to be an omnivore? (Craft and Structure)

3. Turn to page 28. Describe what you think is happening in this photo. Use the text to help with your answer. (Integration of Knowledge and Ideas)

Index